P9-AFE-281

"This slim classic—the West's counterpart to Buddhism's beloved *Dhammapada*—contains more practical wisdom than an entire shelf of today's self-help books. If it seems low-key, that is because Epictetus's grip on the truth is so firm that he doesn't need to raise his voice. Sharon Lebell's deft rendering of the text makes it readily accessible to the contemporary reader."

—Huston Smith, author of *The World's Religions* and *Forgotten Truth*

"In her ingenious rendering, Sharon Lebell has freshly captured the perennial East/West wisdom of Epictetus. In plain, lucid speech, this little book provides a contemporary manual for goodness, composed happiness, moral courage, and inner serenity."

—Willis Barnstone, Distinguished Professor of Comparative Literature, Indiana University

The message of Epictetus is as vital today as it ever was. No other philosopher shows more clearly what it really means to cultivate an active mind in the face of everything that life throws at us. This alone is for many of us the first practical step along the path of inner freedom.

—Jacob Needleman, Professor of Philosophy, San Francisco State University, and author of *The Heart of Philosophy*

A
MANUAL
for
LIVING

EPICTETUS

A New Interpretation by
SHARON LEBELL

HarperSanFrancisco
A Division of HarperCollinsPublishers

About the Editor: Sharon Lebell is a writer and musician who lives in northern California. She is the author of *Naming Ourselves, Naming Our Children.*

Epigraph from Epictetus *Discourses*, 3.23, tr. Thomas W. Higginson (Roslyn, New York: Walter J. Black, 1944), 233.

A MANUAL FOR LIVING. Copyright © 1994 by HarperCollins Publishers. All rights reserved. Printed in the United States of America. No part of this book may be used or reproduced in any manner whatsoever without written permission except in the case of brief quotations embodied in critical articles and reviews. For information address HarperCollins Publishers, 10 East 53rd Street, New York, NY 10022.

Book Design by Ralph Fowler
Set in ITC Berkeley Oldstyle

Library of Congress Cataloging-in-Publication Data
Epictetus.
  [Manual. English]
  A manual for living / Epictetus : a new interpretation by Sharon Lebell.
     p. cm.
  ISBN 0–06–251111–4 (pbk. : alk. paper)
  1. Ethics.   2. Conduct of life.   I. Lebell, Sharon.   II. Title.
  B561.M52E5 1994
  188—dc20
                                                    94–2721
                                                    CIP

03 04 05 06 07 ❖ HAD 17 16 15 14 13

This edition is printed on acid-free paper that meets the American National Standards Institute Z39.48 Standard.

First,
say to yourself
what you would be;
then do what you
have to do.

CONTENTS

PROLOGUE

Part of Epictetus's enduring appeal and widespread influence is that he wasn't fussy about distinguishing between professional philosophers and ordinary people. He expressed his message clearly and zealously to all people interested in living a morally awake life.

Epictetus nevertheless staunchly believed in the necessity of training for the gradual refinement of personal character and behavior. Moral progress is not the natural province of the highborn, nor is it achieved by accident or luck, but by working on yourself—daily.

In keeping with the democratic spirit of Epictetus's doctrine, this small volume encapsulates the great Stoic's key ideas and uses language and imagery suited to our ears today. To present Epictetus's teachings in as straightforward and useful a manner as possible, I have done my share of selection, interpretation, and improvisation with the ideas contained in *The Enchiridion* and *The Discourses*, the only surviving documents that summarize Epictetus's philosophy. My aim has been to communicate the spirit, but not necessarily the letter, of Epictetus. I have thus consulted the various translations of his teachings and then given fresh expression to what I think he would have said today.

Epictetus well understood the eloquence of action. He exhorted his students to shun mere clever theorizing in favor of actively applying his teachings to the concrete circumstances of daily life. Accordingly, I have tried to express the kernels of Epictetus's thought in an up-to-date, provocative way, one that will inspire readers not only to contemplate, but to make the small, successive changes that culminate in personal dignity and a noble life.

THE SPIRIT *of* EPICTETUS

How do I live a happy, fulfilling life?

How can I be a good person?

Answering these two questions was the singled-minded passion of Epictetus, the influential Stoic philosopher who was born a slave about A.D. 55 in Hierapolis, Phrygia, in the eastern outreaches of the Roman Empire.

His teachings, when freed of their ancient cultural trappings, have an uncanny contemporary relevance. At times his philosophy sounds like the best of contemporary psychology. And something like the Serenity Prayer, which epitomizes the recovery movement: "Grant me the serenity to accept the things I cannot change, the courage to change the things I can, and the wisdom to know the difference"—could easily be a sentence in this book. In fact, Epictetus's thought may well be one of the taproots of the modern psychology of self-management, since his teachings have had enormous influence on leading thinkers on the art of living for almost two millennia (even though Epictetus is less known today with the decline of classical education).

In other important ways, Epictetus is very traditional and uncontemporary. Whereas our society, practically if not always explicitly, regards professional achievement, wealth, power, and fame as desirable and admirable, Epictetus views these things as insignificant and irrelevant to true happiness. What matters most is what sort of person you are becoming, what sort of life you are living.

For Epictetus a happy life and a virtuous life are one and the same thing. Happiness and personal fulfillment are the natural consequences of doing the right thing. Unlike many philosophers of his day, Epictetus was less concerned with seeking to understand the world than with identifying the specific steps to take in the pursuit of moral excellence. Part of his genius is his emphasis on moral *progress* over the seeking of moral *perfection*. With a keen understanding of how easily human beings are diverted from living by their highest principles, he exhorts his students to view the philosophical life as a progression of steps that gradually approximate one's cherished personal ideals.

Epictetus's notion of the good life is not a matter of following a laundry list of precepts, but of bringing our actions and desires into harmony with nature. The point is not to perform good deeds to win favor with the gods or the admiration of others, but to achieve inner serenity and thus enduring personal freedom. Goodness is an equal opportunity enterprise, available to *anyone* at any time: rich or poor, educated or simple. It's not the exclusive province of "spiritual professionals" such as monks, saints, or ascetics.

Epictetus advanced a conception of virtue that was simple, ordinary, and day-to-day in its expression. He favored a life lived steadily in accordance with the divine will over extraordinary, conspicuous, heroic displays of goodness.

Epictetus's prescription for the good life centered on three main themes: mastering your desires, performing your duties, and learning to think clearly about yourself and your relations within the larger community of humanity.

Even though Epictetus was a brilliant master of logic and disputation, he didn't flaunt his exceptional rhetorical skill. His demeanor was that of a light-hearted, humble teacher urging his students to take the business of living wisely very seriously. Epictetus walked his talk. He lived modestly in a small hut and eschewed any interest in fame, fortune, and power.

When Epictetus was young, his master, Epaphroditus, Nero's administrative secretary, brought the promising philosopher to Rome. From an early age Epictetus exhibited superior intellectual talent that so impressed Epaphroditus that he sent the young man to study with the famous Stoic teacher, Musonius Rufus. Epictetus became Musonius Rufus's most acclaimed student and was eventually freed from slavery.

Epictetus taught in Rome until A.D. 94 when the emperor Domitian, threatened by the growing influence of philosophers, banished him from Rome. He spent the rest of his life in exile in Nicopolis, on the northwest coast of Greece. There he established a philosophical school and spent his days delivering lectures on how to live with greater dignity and tranquility.

Among his most distinguished students was the young Marcus Aurelius Antoninus, who eventually became ruler of the Roman Empire. He was also the author of the famous *Meditations,* whose Stoic roots were in Epictetus's moral doctrines. Epictetus died about A.D. 135 in Nicopolis.

Invitation to the Manual

Epictetus was a lecturer who himself left no philosophical writings. Fortunately, the main points of his philosophy were preserved for future generations by his devoted pupil, the historian Flavius Arrian. Arrian painstakingly transcribed a large number of his teacher's lectures for a friend. These lectures, known as the *Discourses* (or *Diatribes*), were originally collected in eight books, but only four survive.

Epictetus's *Manual* (or *Enchiridion*) is a pithy set of excerpts selected from the *Discourses* that forms a concise summary of Epictetus's essential teachings. It was roughly modeled on military manuals of the day and thus shares some of the bold simplicity of classics like *The Art of War.* (Soldiers even carried the *Manual* into battle.) Across centuries and cultures, world leaders, generals, and ordinary folk alike have relied on the *Manual* as their main guide to personal serenity and moral direction amid the supreme trials of life.

A
MANUAL
for
LIVING

Know What You Can Control and What You Can't

Happiness and freedom begin with a clear understanding of one principle: some things are within our control, and some things are not. It is only after you have faced up to this fundamental rule and learned to distinguish between what you can and can't control that inner tranquility and outer effectiveness become possible.

Within our control are our own opinions, aspirations, desires, and the things that repel us. These areas are quite rightly our concern, because they are directly subject to our influence. We always have a choice about the contents and character of our inner lives.

Outside our control, however, are such things as what kind of body we have, whether we're born into wealth or strike it rich, how we are regarded by others, and our status in society. We must remember that those things are externals and are therefore not our concern. Trying to control or to change what we can't only results in torment.

Remember: the things within our power are naturally at our disposal, free from any restraint or hindrance; but those things outside our power are weak, dependent, or determined by whims and actions of others. Remember, too, that if you think that you have free rein over things that are naturally beyond your control or if you attempt to adopt the affairs of others as your own, your pursuits will be thwarted and you will become a frustrated, anxious, and fault-finding person.

๑-๑-๑

Stick with Your Own Business

Keep your attention focused entirely on what is truly your own concern and be clear that what belongs to others is their business and none of yours. If you do this, you will be impervious to coercion and no one can ever hold you back. You will be truly free and effective, for your efforts will be put to good use and won't be foolishly squandered finding fault with or opposing others.

In knowing and attending to what actually concerns you, you cannot be made to do anything against your will; others can't hurt you, you don't incur enemies or suffer harm.

If you aim to live by such principles, remember that it won't be easy: you must give up some things entirely, and postpone others for now. You may well have to forego wealth and power if you want to assure the attainment of happiness and freedom.

☙–☙–☙

Recognize Mere Appearances for What They Are

From now on practice saying to everything that appears unpleasant: "You are just an appearance and by no means what you appear to be." And then thoroughly consider the matter according to the principles just discussed, primarily: does this appearance concern the things that are within my own control or those that are not? If it concerns anything outside your control, train yourself not to worry about it.

☙–☙–☙

Desire Demands Its Own Attainment

Our desires and aversions are mercurial rulers. They demand to be pleased. Desire commands us to run off and get what we want. Aversion insists that we must avoid the things that repel us.

Typically, when we don't get what we want, we are disappointed and when we get what we don't want, we are distressed.

If, then, you avoid only those undesirable things that are contrary to your natural well-being and are within your control, you won't ever incur anything you truly don't want. However, if you try to avoid common inevitabilities such as sickness, death, or misfortune, over which you have no real control, you will make yourself and others around you suffer.

Desire and aversion, though powerful, are but habits. And we can train ourselves to have better habits. Restrain the habit of being repelled by all those things that aren't within your control, and focus instead on combating things within your power that are not good for you.

Do your best to rein in your desire. For if you desire something that isn't within your own control, disappointment will surely follow; meanwhile, you will be neglecting the very things that are within your control that are worthy of desire.

Of course, there are times when for practical reasons you must go after one thing or shun another, but do so with grace, finesse, and flexibility.

◦–◦–◦

See Things for What They Really Are

Circumstances do not rise to meet our expectations. Events happen as they do. People behave as they are. Embrace what you actually get.

Open your eyes: see things for what they really are, thereby sparing yourself the pain of false attachments and avoidable devastation.

Think about what delights you—the tools on which you depend, the people whom you cherish. But remember that they have their own distinct character, which is quite a separate matter from how we happen to regard them.

As an exercise, consider the smallest things to which you are attached. For instance, suppose you have a favorite cup. It is, after all, merely a cup, so if it should break, you could cope. Next build up to things—or people—toward which your clinging feelings and thoughts intensify.

Remember, for example, when you embrace your child, your husband, your wife, you are embracing a mortal. Thus, if one of them should die, you could bear it with tranquility.

When something happens, the only thing in your power is your attitude toward it; you can either accept it or resent it.

What really frightens and dismays us is not external events themselves, but the way in which we think about them. It is not things that disturb us, but our *interpretation* of their significance.

Stop scaring yourself with impetuous notions, with your reactive impressions of the way things are!

Things and people are not what we wish them to be or what they seem to be. They are what they are.

⊙-⊙-⊙

Harmonize Your Actions with the Way Life Really Is

Don't try to make your own rules.

Conduct yourself in *all* matters, grand and public or small and domestic, in accordance with the laws of nature. Harmonizing your will with nature should be your utmost ideal.

Where do you practice this ideal? In the particulars of your own daily life with its uniquely personal tasks and duties. When you carry out your tasks, such as taking a bath, do so, to the best of your ability, in harmony with nature. When you eat, do so, to the best of your ability, in harmony with nature, and so on.

It is not so much *what* you are doing as *how* you are doing it. When we properly understand and live by this principle, while difficulties will arise—for they are part of the divine order too—inner peace will still be possible.

❂-❂-❂

Events Don't Hurt Us, But Our Views of Them Can

Things themselves don't hurt or hinder us. Nor do other people. How we view these things is another matter. It is our attitudes and reactions that give us trouble.

Therefore, even death is no big deal in and of itself. It is our notion of death, our idea that it is terrible, that terrifies us. There are so many different ways to think about death. Scrutinize your notions about death—and everything else. Are they really true? Are they doing you any good? Don't dread death or pain; dread the *fear* of death or pain.

We cannot choose our external circumstances, but we can always choose how we respond to them.

⊙-⊙-⊙

No Shame, No Blame

If it is our feelings about things that torment us rather than the things themselves, it follows that blaming others is silly. Therefore, when we suffer setbacks, disturbances, or grief, let us never place the blame on others, but on our own attitudes.

Small-minded people habitually reproach others for their own misfortunes. Average people reproach themselves. Those who are dedicated to a life of wisdom understand that the impulse to blame something or someone is foolishness, that there is nothing to be gained in blaming, whether it be others or oneself.

One of the signs of the dawning of moral progress is the gradual extinguishing of blame. We see the futility of finger-pointing. The more we examine our attitudes and work on ourselves, the less we are apt to be swept away by stormy emotional reactions in which we seek easy explanations for unbidden events.

Things simply are what they are. Other people think what they will think; it is of no concern to us. No Shame. No Blame.

⊙-⊙-⊙

Create Your Own Merit

Never depend on the admiration of others. There is no strength in it. Personal merit cannot be derived from an external source. It is not to be found in your personal associations, nor can it be found in the regard of other people. It is a fact of life that other people, even people who love you, will not necessarily agree with your ideas, understand you, or share your enthusiasms. Grow up! Who cares what other people think about you!

Create your *own* merit.

Personal merit cannot be achieved through our associations with people of excellence. You have been given your own work to do. Get to it right now, do your best at it, and don't be concerned with who is watching you.

Do your own useful work without regard to the honor or admiration your efforts might win from others. There is no such thing as vicarious merit.

Other people's triumphs and excellences belong to them. Likewise, your possessions may have excellence, but you yourself don't derive excellence from them.

Think about it: what is really your own? The *use* you make of the ideas, resources, and opportunities that come your way. Do you have books? Read them. Learn from them. Apply their wisdom. Do you have specialized knowledge? Put it to its full and good use. Do you have tools? Get them out and build or repair things with them. Do you have a good idea? Follow up and follow through on it. Make the most of what you've got, what is actually yours.

You can be justifiably happy with yourself and at ease when you've harmonized your actions with nature by recognizing what truly is your own.

⊙–⊙–⊙

Focus on Your Main Duty

There is a time and place for diversion and amusements, but you should never allow them to override your true purposes. If you were on a voyage and the ship anchored in a harbor, you might go ashore for water and happen to pick up a shellfish or a plant. But be careful; listen for the call of the captain. Keep your attention directed at the ship. Getting distracted by trifles is the easiest thing in the world. Should the captain call, you must be ready to leave those distractions and come running, without even looking back.

If you are old, do not go far from the ship or you might fail to appear when you are called for.

⊙–⊙–⊙

Quietly Accept Events As They Occur

Don't demand that events happen as you would wish them to. Accept events as they actually happen. That way peace is possible.

⊙–⊙–⊙

Your Will Is Always Within Your Power

Nothing truly stops you. Nothing truly holds you back, for your own will is always within your control. Sickness may challenge your body. But are you merely your body?

Lameness may impede your legs. But you are not merely your legs. Your will is bigger than your legs. Your will needn't be affected by an incident unless you let it. Remember this with everything that happens to you.

◉–◉–◉

Make Full Use of What Happens to You

Every difficulty in life presents us with an opportunity to turn inward and to invoke our own inner resources. The trials we endure can and should introduce us to our strengths.

Prudent people look beyond the incident itself and seek to form the habit of putting it to good use.

On the occasion of an accidental event, don't just react in a haphazard fashion: remember to turn inward and ask what resources you have for dealing with it. Dig deeply. You possess strengths you might not realize you have. Find the right one. Use it.

If you encounter an attractive person, then self-restraint is the resource needed; if pain or weakness, then stamina; if verbal abuse, then patience.

As time goes by and you build on the habit of matching the appropriate inner resource to each incident, you will not tend to get carried away by life's appearances. You will stop feeling overwhelmed so much of the time.

⊙–⊛–⊙

Care for What You Happen to Have— There Is Nothing to Lose

Nothing can truly be taken from us. There is nothing to lose. Inner peace begins when we stop saying of things, "I have lost it" and instead say, "It has been returned to where it came from." Has your child died? He or she is returned to where they came from. Has your husband or wife died? He or she is returned to where they came from. Have your possessions and property been taken from you? They too have been returned to where they came from.

Perhaps you are vexed because a bad person took your belongings. But why should it be any concern of yours *who* gives your things back to the world that gave them to you?

The important thing is to take great care with what you have while the world lets you have it, just as a traveler takes care of a room at an inn.

☙☙☙

The Good Life Is the Life of Inner Serenity

The surest sign of the higher life is serenity. Moral progress results in freedom from inner turmoil. You can stop fretting about this and that.

If you seek the higher life, refrain from such common patterns of thinking as these: "If I don't work harder, I'll never earn a decent living, no one will recognize me, I'll be a nobody" or "If I don't criticize my employee, he'll take advantage of my good will."

It's much better to die of hunger unhindered by grief and fear than to live affluently beset with worry, dread, suspicion, and unchecked desire.

Begin at once a program of self-mastery. But start modestly, with the little things that bother you.

Has your child spilled something? Have you misplaced your wallet? Say to yourself, "Coping calmly with this inconvenience is the price I pay for my inner serenity, for freedom from perturbation; you don't get something for nothing."

When you call your child, be prepared that she may not respond to you, or if she does, she might not do what you want her to do. Under these circumstances, it doesn't help your child for you to become agitated. It should not be in her power to cause you any disturbance.

Pay No Attention to Things That Don't Concern You

Spiritual progress requires us to highlight what is essential and to disregard everything else as trivial pursuits unworthy of our attention. Moreover, it is actually a good thing to be thought foolish and simple with regard to matters that don't concern us. Don't be concerned with other people's impressions of you. They are dazzled and deluded by appearances. Stick with *your* purpose. This alone will strengthen your will and give your life coherence.

Refrain from trying to win other people's approval and admiration. You are taking a higher road. Don't long for others to see you as sophisticated, unique, or wise. In fact, be suspicious if you appear to others as someone special. Be on your guard against a false sense of self-importance.

Keeping your will in harmony with truth and concerning yourself with what is beyond your control are mutually exclusive. While you are absorbed in one, you will neglect the other.

◉◉◉

Conform Your Wants and Expectations to Reality

For good or for ill, life and nature are governed by laws that we can't change. The quicker we accept this, the more tranquil we can be. You would be foolish to wish that your children or your spouse would live forever. They are mortal, just as you are, and the law of mortality is completely out of your hands.

Similarly, it is foolish to wish that an employee, relative, or friend be without fault. This is wishing to control things that you can't truly control.

It is within our control not to be disappointed by our desires if we deal with them according to facts rather than by being swept away by them.

We are ultimately controlled by that which bestows or removes what we seek or avoid. If it's freedom you seek, then wish nothing and shun nothing that depends on others, or you will always be a helpless slave.

Understand what freedom really is and how it is achieved. Freedom isn't the right or ability to do whatever you please. Freedom comes from understanding the limits of our own power and the natural limits set in place by divine providence. By accepting life's limits and inevitabilities and working with them rather than fighting them, we become free. If, on the other hand, we succumb to our passing desires for things that aren't in our control, freedom is lost.

☺-☺-☺

Approach Life As If It Were a Banquet

Think of your life as if it were a banquet where you would behave graciously. When dishes are passed to you, extend your hand and help yourself to a moderate portion. If a dish should pass you by, enjoy what is already on your plate. Or if the dish hasn't been passed to you yet, patiently wait your turn.

Carry over this same attitude of polite restraint and gratitude to your children, spouse, career, and finances. There is no need to yearn, envy, and grab. You will get your rightful portion when it is your time.

Diogenes and Heraclitus were impeccable models of living by such principles rather than by raw impulses. Make it your quest to imitate their worthy example.

☺-☺-☺

Avoid Adopting Other People's Negative Views

Other people's views and troubles can be contagious. Don't sabotage yourself by unwittingly adopting negative, unproductive attitudes through your associations with others.

If you encounter a downhearted friend, a grieving parent, or a colleague who has suffered a sudden reversal of fortune, be careful not to be overcome yourself by the apparent misfortune. Remember to discriminate between events themselves and our interpretations of them. Remind yourself: "What hurts this person is not the occurrence itself, for another person might not feel oppressed by this situation at all. What is hurting this person is the response he or she has uncritically adopted."

It is not a demonstration of kindness or friendship to the people we care about to join them in indulging in wrongheaded, negative feelings. We do a better service to ourselves and others by remaining detached and avoiding melodramatic reactions.

Still, if you find yourself in conversation with someone who is depressed, hurt, or frustrated, show them kindness and give them a sympathetic ear; just don't allow yourself to be pulled down too.

◉-◉-◉

Always Act Well the Part That Is Given to You

We are like actors in a play. The divine will has assigned us our roles in life without consulting us. Some of us will act in a short drama, others in a long one. We might be assigned the part of a poor person, a cripple, a distinguished celebrity or public leader, or an ordinary private citizen.

Although we can't control which roles are assigned to us, it must be our business to act our given role as best as we possibly can and to refrain from complaining about it. Wherever you find yourself and in whatever circumstances, give an impeccable performance.

If you are supposed to be a reader, read; if you are supposed to be a writer, write.

Everything Happens for a Good Reason

As you think, so you become. Avoid superstitiously investing events with power or meanings they don't have. Keep your head. Our busy minds are forever jumping to conclusions, manufacturing and interpreting signs that aren't there.

Assume, instead, that everything that happens to you does so for some good. That if you decided to be lucky, you are lucky. All events contain an advantage for you—if you look for it!

⊙-⊙-⊙

Happiness Can Only Be Found Within

Freedom is the only worthy goal in life. It is won by disregarding things that lie beyond our control. We cannot have a light heart if our minds are a woeful cauldron of fear and ambition.

Do you wish to be invincible? Then don't enter into combat with what you have no real control over. Your happiness depends on three things, all of which are within your power: your will, your ideas concerning the events in which you are involved, and the use you make of your ideas.

Authentic happiness is always independent of external conditions. Vigilantly practice indifference to external conditions. Your happiness can only be found within.

How easily dazzled and deceived we are by eloquence, job title, degrees, high honors, fancy possessions, expensive clothing, or a suave demeanor. Don't make the mistake of assuming that celebrities, public figures, political leaders, the wealthy, or people with great intellectual or artistic gifts are necessarily happy. To do so is to be bewildered by appearances and will only make you doubt yourself.

Remember: the real essence of good is found only within things under your own control. If you keep this in mind, you won't find yourself feeling falsely envious or forlorn, pitifully comparing yourself and your accomplishments to others.

Stop aspiring to be anyone other than your own best self: for that *does* fall within your control.

☯-☯-☯

No One Can Hurt You

People don't have the power to hurt you. Even if someone shouts abuse at you or strikes you, if you are insulted, it is always your choice to view what is happening as insulting or not. If someone irritates you, it is only your own response that is irritating you. Therefore, when anyone seems to be provoking you, remember that it is only your judgment of the incident that provokes you. Don't let your emotions get ignited by mere appearances.

Try not to merely react in the moment. Pull back from the situation. Take a wider view; compose yourself.

☙–☙–☙

Spiritual Progress Is Made Through Confronting Death and Calamity

Instead of averting your eyes from the painful events of life, look at them squarely and contemplate them often. By facing the realities of death, infirmity, loss, and disappointment, you free yourself of illusions and false hopes and you avoid miserable, envious thoughts.

⊙-⊙-⊙

Implant in Yourself the Ideals You Ought to Cherish

Attach yourself to what is spiritually superior, regardless of what other people think or do. Hold to your true aspirations no matter what is going on around you.

⊙-⊙-⊙

Those Who Seek a Life of Wisdom Will Be Ridiculed

Those who pursue the higher life of wisdom, who seek to live by spiritual principles, must be prepared to be laughed at and condemned.

Many people who have progressively lowered their personal standards in an attempt to win social acceptance and life's comforts bitterly resent those of philosophical bent who refuse to compromise their spiritual ideals and who seek to better themselves. Never live your life in reaction to these poor souls. Be compassionate toward them, and at the same time hold to what *you* know is good.

When you begin your program of spiritual progress, chances are the people close to you will deride you and accuse you of arrogance.

It is your job to comport yourself humbly and to consistently hew to your moral ideals. Cling to what you know in your heart is best. Then, if you are steadfast, the very people who ridiculed you will come to admire you.

But if you allow the mean-spirited opinions of others to make you waver in your purpose, you incur a double shame.

☉–☉–☉

Seeking to Please Others Is a Perilous Trap

In trying to please other people, we find ourselves misdirected toward what lies outside our sphere of influence. In doing so we lose our hold on our life's purpose.

Content yourself with being a lover of wisdom, a seeker of the truth. Return and return again to what is essential and worthy.

Do not try to seem wise to others.

If you want to live a wise life, live it on your own terms and in your own eyes.

☙☙☙

Character Matters More Than Reputation

Worry and dread are a waste of time and do not set a good example for others. This is especially true regarding your reputation and influence. Why live in fear about things such as whether you will gain public recognition in your profession or community? Or whether you will get the opportunities and perquisites that others do?

Don't be bothered by such concerns as "People don't think well of me, and I'm a nobody." Even if your reputation were really to matter, you're not responsible for what others think of you. What real difference does it make to your character and well-being if you have a powerful position or get invited to fancy parties? None at all. So how is there any discredit in not being a power broker or a celebrity? And why should you worry about being a nobody when what matters is being a somebody in those areas of your life over which you have control and in which you can make a real difference?

"But without power and repute I won't be able to help my friends," you might say. It's true that you won't give them access to money or the halls of power. But who really expects that such assistance is yours to give and not for others to provide? Who can be expected to give anything that they don't have? "Still, it would be great to have money and power and to be able to share them with my friends." If I can get rich and powerful while preserving my own honor, faithfulness to family, friends, principles, and self-respect, show me how and I'll do it. But if I have to sacrifice my personal integrity, it's stupid and silly to urge me on. Besides, if you had to choose between having a certain amount of money and having a loyal and honorable friend, which would you choose? It's better if you help me become a good person than to push me to do things that threaten my good character.

"Well, what about my obligations to my country?" What do you mean? If you're talking about making grand charitable donations or putting up fancy buildings, is that really an issue? A metalworker doesn't make shoes, and a shoemaker doesn't make weapons. It is enough if everyone does well what he or she is supposed to do. "Well, what if someone else were to do the same thing as me?" That's fine. It doesn't make your contribution any less valuable. "But what about my position in society?" you ask. Whatever position you can hold while preserving your honor and your fidelity to your obligations is fine. But if your desire to contribute to society compromises your moral responsibility, how can you serve your fellow citizens when you've become irresponsible and shameless?

It's better to be a good person and fulfill your obligations than to have renown and power.

☙☙☙

All Advantages Have Their Price

Is someone enjoying the privileges, opportunities, or honor you desire? If the advantages they've secured are good, then delight in that person enjoying them. It is his or her time to prosper. If those advantages are bad, then don't be troubled that they didn't come your way.

Remember: you will never earn the same rewards as others without employing the same methods and investment of time as they do. It is unreasonable to think we can earn rewards without being willing to pay their true price. The person who "wins" at something has no real advantage over you, because they had to pay the price for the reward.

It is always our choice whether or not we wish to pay the price for life's rewards. And often it is best for us not to pay the price, for the price might buy our integrity. We could be forced to praise someone whom we don't respect.

☙—☙—☙

Make the Will of
Nature Your Own

Learn the will of nature. Study it, pay attention to it, and then make it your own.

The will of nature is revealed to us through experiences common to all people. For example, if a neighbor's child breaks a bowl, or some similar thing, we readily say, "These things happen." When your own bowl breaks, you should respond in the same way as when another person's bowl breaks.

Carry this understanding over to matters of greater emotional import and worldly consequence. Has the child or spouse or other dear one of another person died? Under such circumstances, there is no one who would not say, "Such is the cycle of life. Death happens. Some things are inevitable."

But if our own child or dearly beloved dies, we tend to cry out, "Woe is me! How miserable I am!"

Remember how you feel when you hear the same thing concerning other people. Transfer that feeling to your own current circumstances. Learn to accept events, even death, with intelligence.

☙❧❧

Self-Mastery Is the Target That the Divine Will Wishes Us to Aim At

Evil does not naturally dwell in the world, in events, or in people. Evil is a by-product of forgetfulness, laziness, or distraction: it arises when we lose sight of our true aim in life.

When we remember that our aim is spiritual progress, we return to striving to be our best selves. This is how happiness is won.

⊙-⊙-⊙

Treasure Your Mind, Cherish Your Reason, Hold to Your Purpose

Don't surrender your mind.

If someone were to casually give your body away to any old passerby, you would naturally be furious.

Why then do you feel no shame in giving your precious mind over to any person who might wish to influence you? Think twice before you give up your own mind to someone who may revile you, leaving you confused and upset.

⊙-⊙-⊙

Consider What Comes First, Then What Follows, and Then Act

Cultivate the habit of surveying and testing a prospective action before undertaking it. Before you proceed, step back and look at the big picture, lest you act rashly on raw impulse. Determine what happens first, consider what that leads to, and then act in accordance with what you've learned.

When we act without circumspection, we might begin a task with great enthusiasm; then when unforeseen or unwanted consequences follow, we shamefully retreat and are filled with regret: "I *would* have done this; I *could* have done that; I *should* have done it differently."

Suppose you wanted to be victorious at the Olympic Games. That's fine, but fully consider what you're getting yourself into. What does such a desire entail? What needs to happen first? Then what? What will be required of you? And what else follows from that? Is this whole course of action really beneficial to you? If so, carry on.

If you wish to win at the Olympic Games, to prepare yourself properly you would have to follow a strict regimen that stretches you to the limits of your endurance. You would have to submit to demanding rules, follow a suitable diet, stay away from candy and desserts, vigorously exercise at a regular time in both heat and cold, and give up drinking. You would have to follow the directions of your trainer as if he or she were your doctor. Then, once you are actually in competition, there's a good chance you'd be hurled into a ditch. You might injure your arm, sprain your ankle, get your face slammed in the mud; and after going through all this, you might still be defeated.

After you have contemplated all these possibilities—mindful of all the things that might happen and their consequences—and if your resolve is still strong, then exercise your judgment. If the overall picture still seems beneficial, then do enter the Games—wholeheartedly.

By considering the big picture, you distinguish yourself from the mere dabbler, the person who plays at things as long as they feel comfortable or interesting. This is not noble. Think things through and fully commit! Otherwise, you will be like a child who sometimes pretends he's a wrestler, sometimes a soldier, sometimes a musician, sometimes an actor in a tragedy.

Unless we fully give ourselves over to our endeavors, we are hollow, superficial people and we never develop our natural gifts. We've all known people who, like monkeys, mimic whatever seems novel and flashy at the moment. But then their enthusiasm and efforts wane; they drop their projects as soon as they become too familiar or demanding.

A half-hearted spirit has no power. Tentative efforts lead to tentative outcomes. Average people enter into their endeavors headlong and without care. Perhaps they meet with an exemplary figure like Euphrates and become inspired to excel themselves. It is all well and good to do this, but consider first the real nature of your aspirations, and measure that against your capacities.

Be honest with yourself. Clearly assess your strengths and weaknesses. Do you have what it takes to compete at this time? To be a wrestler, for instance, requires extraordinary strength in one's shoulders, back, and thighs. Do you have the physical prowess and agility to be among the best in this sport? It is one thing to wish to be a champion or to do something skillfully; it is another to actually do it and to do it with consummate skill. Different people are made for different things.

Just as certain capacities are required for success in a particular area, so too are certain sacrifices required. If you wish to become proficient in the art of living with wisdom, do you think that you can eat and drink to excess? Do you think you can continue to succumb to anger and your usual habits of frustration and unhappiness? No. If true wisdom is your object and you are sincere, you will have work to do on yourself. You will have to overcome many unhealthy cravings and knee-jerk reactions. You will have to reconsider whom you associate with. Are your friends and associates worthy people? Does their influence—their habits, values, and behavior—

elevate you or reinforce the slovenly habits from which you seek escape? The life of wisdom, like anything else, demands its price. You may, in following it, be ridiculed and even end up with the worst of everything in all parts of your public life, including your career, your social standing, and your legal position in the courts.

Once you have given due consideration to all of the constituent details that compose the effort to live the higher life, venture forth with your utmost effort. Make the necessary sacrifices that are the price for the worthiest of goals: freedom, evenmindedness, and tranquility. If, however, upon honestly appraising your mettle, you are not fit or ready, free yourself from delusion and tread a different, more realistic road.

If you try to be something you're not or strive for something completely beyond your present capacities, you end up as a pathetic dabbler, trying first to be a wise person, then a bureaucrat, then a politician, then a civic leader. These roles are not consistent. You can't be flying off in countless directions, however appealing they are, and at the same time live an integrated, fruitful life.

You can only be one person—either a good person or a bad person. You have two essential choices. Either you can set yourself to developing your reason, cleaving to truth, or you can hanker after externals. The choice is yours and yours alone. You can either put your skills toward internal work or lose yourself to externals, which is to say, be a person of wisdom, or follow the common ways of the mediocre.

⊙─⊙─⊙

Our Duties Are Revealed by Our Relations with One Another

You are not an isolated entity, but a unique, irreplaceable part of the cosmos. Don't forget this. You are an essential piece of the puzzle of humanity. Each of us is a part of a vast, intricate, and perfectly ordered human community. But where do you fit into this web of humanity? To whom are you beholden?

Look for and come to understand your connections to other people. We properly locate ourselves within the cosmic scheme by recognizing our natural relations to one another and thereby identifying our duties. Our duties naturally emerge from such fundamental relations as our families, neighborhoods, workplaces, our state or nation. Make it your regular habit to consider your roles—parent, child, neighbor, citizen, leader—and the natural duties that arise from them. Once you know who you are and to whom you are linked, you will know what to do.

If a man is your father, for instance, certain emotional and practical claims follow from this. That he is your father implies a fundamental, durable link between the two of you. You are naturally obligated to care for him, to listen to his advice, to exercise patience in hearing his views, and to respect his guidance.

However, let us suppose that he's not a good father. Perhaps he is fatuous, uneducated, unrefined, or holds views quite different from your own. Does nature give everyone an *ideal* father, or simply a father? When it comes to your fundamental duty as a son or daughter, whatever your father's character may be, whatever his personality or habits are, is secondary. The divine order does not design people or circumstance according to our tastes. Whether you find him to be agreeable or not, this man is, when all is said and done, your father, and you should live up to all your filial obligations.

Suppose you have a brother or sister who treats you poorly. What difference does that make? There is still a moral imperative to recognize and maintain your fundamental duty to him or her. Focus not on what he or she does, but on keeping to *your* higher purpose. Your own purpose should seek harmony with nature itself. For this is the true road to freedom. Let others behave as they will—that is not within your control anyway, and thus it's of no concern to you. Understand that nature as a whole is ordered according to reason, but that not everything in nature is reasonable.

When you are faithfully occupied with performing the acts of a wise and decent person, seeking to conform your intentions and acts to the divine will, you do not feel victimized by the words or deeds of others. At worst, those words and deeds will seem amusing or pitiable.

Except for extreme physical abuse, other people cannot hurt you unless you allow them to. And this holds true even if the person is your parent, brother, sister, teacher, or employer. Don't consent to be hurt and you won't be hurt—this *is* a choice over which you have control.

Most people tend to delude themselves into thinking that freedom comes from doing what feels good or what fosters comfort and ease. The truth is that people who subordinate reason to their feelings of the moment are actually slaves of their desires and aversions. They are ill-prepared to act effectively and nobly when unexpected challenges occur, as they inevitably will.

Authentic freedom places demands on us. In discovering and comprehending our fundamental relations to one another and zestfully performing our duties, true freedom, which all people long for, is indeed possible.

☙☙☙

The Essence of Faithfulness

The essence of faithfulness lies first in holding correct opinions and attitudes toward the Ultimate. Remember that the divine order is intelligent and fundamentally good. Life is not a series of random, meaningless episodes, but an ordered, elegant whole that follows ultimately comprehensible laws.

The divine will exists and directs the universe with justice and goodness. Though it is not always apparent if you merely look at the surface of things, the universe we inhabit is the best possible universe.

Fix your resolve on expecting justice and goodness and order, and they will increasingly reveal themselves to you in all your affairs. Trust that there is a divine intelligence whose intentions direct the universe. Make it your utmost goal to steer your life in accordance with the will of divine order.

When you strive to conform your intentions and actions with the divine order, you don't feel persecuted, helpless, confused, or resentful toward the circumstances of your life. You will feel strong, purposeful, and sure.

Faithfulness is not blind belief; it consists of steadfastly practicing the principle of shunning those things which are not within your control, leaving them to be worked out according to the natural system of responsibilities. Cease trying to anticipate or control events. Instead accept them with grace and intelligence.

It is impossible to remain faithful to your ordained purpose if you drift into imagining that those things outside your power are inherently good or evil. When this happens the habit of blaming outside factors for our lot in life inevitably sets in, and we lose ourselves in a negative spiral of envy, strife, disappointment, anger, and reproach. For by nature all creatures recoil from the things they think would do them harm and seek out and admire those things that seem good and helpful.

The second aspect of faithfulness is the importance of prudently observing the customs of your family, your country, and local community. Perform your community's rituals with a pure heart, without greed or extravagance. In doing so, you join the spiritual order of your people and further the ultimate aspirations of humanity.

Faithfulness is the antidote to bitterness and confusion and it confers the conviction that we are ready for anything the divine will intends for us. Your aim should be to view the world as an integrated whole, to faithfully incline your whole being toward the highest good, and to adopt the will of nature as your own.

☯-☯-☯

Events Themselves Are Impersonal and Indifferent

When considering the future, remember that all situations unfold as they do regardless of how we feel about them. Our hopes and fears sway us, not events themselves.

Undisciplined people, driven by their personal antipathies and sympathies, are forever on the lookout for signs that build up or reinforce their unexamined views and opinions. Yet events themselves are impersonal, though judicious people certainly can and should respond to them in beneficial ways.

Instead of personalizing an event ("this is *my* triumph, that was *his* blunder, or this is *my* bitter misfortune") and drawing withering conclusions about yourself or human nature, watch for how you can put certain aspects of the event to good use. Is there some less-than-obvious benefit embedded in the event that a trained eye might discern? Pay attention; be a sleuth. Perhaps there is a lesson you can extract and apply to similar events in the future.

In *all* events, however seemingly dire, there is nothing to prevent us from searching for its hidden opportunity. It is a failure of the imagination not to do so. But to seek out the opportunity in situations requires a great deal of courage, for most people around you will persist in interpreting events in the grossest terms: success or failure, good or bad, right or wrong. These simplistic, polarized categories obscure more creative—and *useful*—interpretations of events that are far more advantageous and interesting!

The wise person knows it is fruitless to project your hopes and fears on the future. This only leads to forming melodramatic representations in your mind and wasting time.

At the same time, one shouldn't passively acquiesce to the future and what it holds. Simply doing nothing does not avoid risk, but heightens it.

There is a place for prudent planning and for making provision for situations to come. Proper preparation for the future consists of forming good personal habits. This is done by actively pursuing the good in all the particulars of your daily life and by regularly examining your motives to make sure they are free of the shackles of fear, greed, and laziness. If you do this, you won't be buffeted about by outside events.

Train your *intentions* rather than fooling yourself into thinking you can manipulate outside events. If you are helped by praying or meditating, by all means do so. But seek divine counsel when the application of your own reason hasn't yielded any answers, when you have exhausted other means.

What is a "good" event? What is a "bad" event? There is no such thing! What is a good person? The one who achieves tranquility by having formed the habit of asking on every occasion, "what is the right thing to do now?"

☯-☯-☯

Never Suppress a Generous Impulse

Follow through on all your generous impulses. Do not question them, especially if a friend needs you; act on his or her behalf. Do not hesitate!

Don't sit around speculating about the possible problems or dangers. As long as you let your reason lead the way, you will be safe.

It is our duty to stand by our friends in their hour of need.

☯-☯-☯

Clearly Define the Person You Want to Be

Who exactly do you want to be? What kind of person do you want to be? What are your personal ideals? Whom do you admire? What are their special traits that you would make your own?

It's time to stop being vague. If you wish to be an extraordinary person, if you wish to be wise, then you should explicitly identify the kind of person you aspire to become. If you have a daybook, write down who you're trying to be, so that you can refer to this self-definition. Precisely describe the demeanor you want to adopt so that you may preserve it when you are by yourself or with other people.

☯-☯-☯

Speak Only with Good Purpose

So much attention is given to the moral importance of our deeds and their effects. Those who seek to live the higher life also come to understand the oft-ignored moral power of our words.

One of the clearest marks of the moral life is right speech. Perfecting our speech is one of the keystones of an authentic spiritual program.

First and foremost, think *before* you speak to make sure you are speaking with good purpose. Glib talk disrespects others. Breezy self-disclosure disrespects yourself. So many people feel compelled to give voice to any passing feeling, thought, or impression they have. They randomly dump the contents of their minds without regard to the consequences. This is practically and morally dangerous. If we babble about every idea that occurs to us—big and small—we can easily fritter away in the trivial currents of mindless talk ideas that have true merit. Unchecked speech is like a vehicle wildly lurching out of control and destined for a ditch.

If need be, be mostly silent or speak sparingly. Speech itself is neither good nor evil, but it is so commonly used carelessly, that you need to be on your guard. Frivolous talk is hurtful talk; besides, it is unbecoming to be a chatterbox.

Enter into discussions when social or professional occasion calls for it, but be cautious that the spirit and intent of the discussion and its content remain worthy. Prattle is seductive. Stay out of its clutches.

It's not necessary to restrict yourself to lofty subjects or philosophy all the time, but be aware that the common babbling that passes for worthwhile discussion has a corrosive effect on your higher purpose. When we blather about trivial things, we ourselves become trivial, for our attention gets taken up with trivialities. You become what you give your attention to.

We become small-minded if we engage in discussion about other people. In particular, avoid blaming, praising, or comparing people.

Try whenever possible, if you notice the conversation around you decaying into palaver, to see if you can subtly lead the conversation back to more constructive subjects. If, however, you find yourself among indifferent strangers, you can simply remain silent.

Be of good humor and enjoy a good laugh when it is apt, but avoid the kind of unrestrained barroom laughter that easily degenerates into vulgarity or malevolence. Laugh *with,* but never laugh *at.*

If you can, avoid making idle promises whenever possible.

☙—☙—☙

Stay Away from Most Popular Entertainment

Most of what passes for legitimate entertainment is inferior or foolish and only caters to or exploits people's weaknesses. Avoid being one of the mob who indulges in such pastimes. Your life is too short and you have important things to do. Be discriminating about what images and ideas you permit into your mind. If you yourself don't choose what thoughts and images you expose yourself to, someone else will, and their motives may not be the highest. It is the easiest thing in the world to slide imperceptibly into vulgarity. But there's no need for that to happen if you determine not to waste your time and attention on mindless pap.

☙—☙—☙

Be Careful About the Company You Keep

Regardless of what others profess, they may not truly live by spiritual values. Be careful whom you associate with. It is human to imitate the habits of those with whom we interact. We inadvertently adopt their interests, their opinions, their values, and their habit of interpreting events. Though many people mean well, they can just the same have a deleterious influence on you because they are undisciplined about what is worthy and what isn't.

Just because some people are nice to you doesn't mean you should spend time with them. Just because they seek you out and are interested in you or your affairs doesn't mean you should associate with them. Be selective about whom you take on as friends, colleagues, and neighbors. All of these people can have an effect on your destiny. The world is full of agreeable and talented folk. The key is to keep company only with people who uplift you, whose presence calls forth your best. But remember that our moral influence is a two-way street, and we should thus make sure by our own thoughts, words, and deeds to be a positive influence on those we deal with. The real test of personal excellence lies in the attention we give to the often neglected small details of our conduct.

Regularly ask yourself, "How are my thoughts, words, and deeds affecting my friends, my spouse, my neighbor, my child, my employer, my subordinates, my fellow citizens? Am I doing my part to contribute to the spiritual progress of all with whom I come in contact?" Make it your business to draw out the best in others by being an exemplar yourself.

◉-◉-◉

Take Care of Your Body, But Don't Show It Off

Respect your body's needs. Give your body excellent care to promote its health and well-being. Give it everything it absolutely requires, including healthy food and drink, dignified clothing, and a warm and comfortable home. Do not, however, use your body as an occasion for show or luxury.

◉-◉-◉

Avoid Casual Sex

Abstain from casual sex and particularly avoid sexual intercourse before you get married. This sounds prudish, but it is a time-tested way by which we demonstrate respect for ourselves and others.

If, however, you know someone who has had casual sex, don't self-righteously try to win them over to your own views.

☙─☙─☙

Refrain from Defending Your Reputation or Intentions

Don't be afraid of verbal abuse or criticism.

Only the morally weak feel compelled to defend or explain themselves to others. Let the quality of your deeds speak on your behalf. We can't control the impressions others form about us, and the effort to do so only debases our character.

So, if anyone should tell you that a particular person has spoken critically of you, don't bother with excuses or defenses. Just smile and reply, "I guess that person doesn't know about all my other faults. Otherwise he wouldn't have mentioned only these."

⊙-⊙-⊙

Conduct Yourself with Dignity

No matter where you find yourself, comport your-self as if you were a distinguished person.

While the behavior of many people is dictated by what is going on around them, hold yourself to a higher standard. Take care to avoid parties or games where thoughtless revelry and carousing are the norm. If you find yourself at a public event, remain rooted in your own purposes and ideals.

⊙-⊙-⊙

Embody Your Personal Ideals by Emulating Role Models

One of the best ways to elevate your character im-mediately is to find worthy role models to emulate. If you have the opportunity to meet with an important person, don't be nervous. Invoke the characteristics of the people you admire most and adopt their manners, speech, and behavior as your own. There is nothing false in this. We all carry the seeds of greatness within us, but we need an image as a point of focus in order that they may sprout.

At the same time, just because you are meeting a person of great merit doesn't mean you should be overly awed. People are just people, regardless of their talent or influence.

☙☙☙

Exercise Discretion When Conversing

Self-importance is not the way of the true philosopher. Nobody enjoys the company of a braggart. Therefore, don't oppress people with dramatic stories of your own exploits. Nobody cares that much about your war stories and dramatic adventures, though they might indulge you for a while to appear polite. To speak frequently and excessively of your own achievements is tiresome and pompous.

You don't need to be the class clown. Nor do you need to resort to other indelicate methods in order to convince others you are clever, sophisticated, or affable.

Aggressive, glib, or showy talk should be completely avoided. It just lowers you in the esteem of your acquaintances.

Many people casually pepper their speech with obscenities in an attempt to bring force and intensity to their speech or to embarrass others. Refuse to go along with such talk. When people around you start to slip into indecent, pointless speech, leave if you can, or at least be silent and let your look of seriousness show that you are offended by such coarse talk.

☙—☙—☙

Prefer Enduring Satisfaction to Immediate Gratification

Let your reason be supreme.
Inculcate the habit of deliberation.

Practice the art of testing whether particular things are actually good or not. Learn to wait and assess instead of always reacting from untrained instinct. Spontaneity is not a virtue in and of itself.

If some pleasure is promised to you and it seductively calls to you, step back and give yourself some time before mindlessly jumping at it. Dispassionately turn the matter over in your mind: Will this pleasure bring but a momentary delight, or real, lasting satisfaction? It makes a difference in the quality of our life and the kind of person we become when we learn how to distinguish between cheap thrills and meaningful, lasting rewards.

If, in calmly considering this pleasure, you realize that if you indulge in it you will regret it, abstain and rejoice in your forbearance. Reinforce the triumph of your character and you will be strengthened.

⊙-⊙-⊙

Take a Stand

Once you have deliberated and determined that a course of action is wise, never try to discredit your judgment. Stand behind your decision. Chances are there may indeed be people who misunderstand your intentions and who may even condemn you. But if, according to your best judgment, you are acting rightly, you have nothing to fear. Take a stand. Don't be cravenly noncommittal.

⊙-⊙-⊙

Common Courtesy and Logic Each Have Their Place

Propriety and logic are different things and each has its appropriate application.

The proposition "either it is day or it is night" works well in a disjunctive argument, but not as well in a friendly conversation. Likewise, at a banquet it may make sense to take the largest share of food if you are really hungry, but it would be bad manners to do so.

When you dine with others, be aware not only how much your body appreciates the delicacies offered, but also how important good manners and personal refinement are.

�⊙-☺-⊙

Self-Mastery Depends on Self-Honesty

Know first who you are and what you're capable of. Just as nothing great is created instantly, the same goes for the perfecting of our talents and aptitudes. We are always learning, always growing. It is right to accept challenges. This is how we progress to the next level of intellectual, physical, or moral development. Still, don't kid yourself: if you try to be something or someone you are not, you belittle your true self and end up not developing in those areas that you would have excelled at quite naturally.

Within the divine order we each have our own special calling. Listen to yours and follow it faithfully.

◑-◉-◐

Safeguard Your Reason

Just as when you walk you are careful not to step on a nail or injure your foot, you should similarly take the utmost care not to in any way impair the highest faculty of your mind. The virtuous life depends on reason first and foremost. If you safeguard your reason, it will safeguard you.

◑-◉-◐

Observe Proper Proportion and Moderation

Through vigilance we can forestall the tendency to excess. A person's possessions should be proportionate to the needs of his or her body, just as the shoe should fit the foot.

Without moral training, we can be induced to excess. In the case of shoes, for instance, many people are tempted to buy fancy, exotic shoes when all that is needed is comfortable, well-fitting, durable footwear.

Once we fall, however slightly, into immoderation, momentum gathers and we can be lost to whim.

☙—☙—☙

Decency and Inner Beauty Are More Valuable Than Appearance

Females are especially burdened by the attention they receive for their pleasing appearance. From the time they are young, they are flattered by males or evaluated only in terms of their outward appearance.

Unfortunately, this can make a woman feel suited only to give men pleasure, and her true inner gifts sadly atrophy. She may feel compelled to put great effort and time into enhancing her outer beauty and distorting her natural self to please others.

Sadly, many people—both men and women—place all their emphasis on managing their physical appearance and the impression they make on others.

Those who seek wisdom come to understand that even though the world may reward us for wrong or superficial reasons, such as our physical appearance, the family we come from, and so on, what really matters is who we are inside and who we are becoming.

☻-☻-☻

Your Reason Is More Important Than Your Body

Those who are morally untrained spend an inordinate amount of time on their bodies. Carry out your animal functions incidentally. Your main attention should be given to the care and development of your reason. For through your reason you are able to understand nature's laws.

☻-☻-☻

Mistreatment Comes from
False Impressions

If someone treats you disrespectfully or speaks unkindly about you, remember that he or she does so from their impression that it is right to do so.

It is unrealistic to expect that this person sees you as you see yourself. If another person reaches conclusions based on false impressions, he or she is the one hurt rather than you, because it is that person who is misguided. When someone interprets a true proposition as a false one, the proposition itself isn't hurt; only the person who holds the wrong view is deceived, and thus damaged. Once you clearly understand this, you will be less likely to feel affronted by others, even if they revile you. You can say to yourself, "It seemed so to that person, but that is only their impression."

Everything Has Two Handles

Everything has two handles: one by which it may be carried, the other by which it can't.

If, for example, your brother or sister treats you poorly, don't grasp the situation by the handle of hurt or injustice, or you won't be able to bear it and you will become bitter. Do the opposite. Grasp the situation by the handle of familial ties. In other words, focus on the fact that this is your brother or sister, that you were brought up together, and thus have an enduring, unbreakable bond. Viewing the situation that way, you understand it correctly and preserve your equilibrium.

☻-☻-☻

Clear Thinking Is Vital

The life of wisdom is a life of reason. It is important to learn how to think clearly. Clear thinking is not a haphazard enterprise. It requires proper training. It is through clear thinking that we are able to properly direct our will, stick with our true purpose, and discover the connections we have to others and the duties that follow from those relationships. Every person should learn how to identify mushy and fallacious thinking. Study how inferences are legitimately derived, so that you avoid drawing unfounded conclusions.

For instance, note the following examples of faulty logic: "I am richer than you; therefore, I am better than you." One encounters such absurd assertions as this all the time, but they are completely fallacious. The valid inference that can be drawn is this: "I am richer than you; therefore, I have more possessions or money than you do."

Another example: "I speak more persuasively than you; therefore, I am better than you." From this we can only conclude, "I speak more persuasively than you; therefore, my speech carries more effect than yours."

But remember: your character is independent of property or persuasive speech.

Take the time to assiduously study clear thinking and you won't be hoodwinked. Strong education in logic and the rules of effective argument will serve you well.

☺-☺-☺

Call Things by Their Right Names

When we name things correctly, we comprehend them correctly, without adding information or judgments that aren't there. Does someone bathe quickly? Don't say he bathes poorly, but quickly. Name the situation as it is; don't filter it through your judgments.

Does someone drink a lot of wine? Don't say he is a drunk but that he drinks a lot. Unless you possess a comprehensive understanding of his life, how do you know if he is a drunk?

Do not risk being beguiled by appearances and constructing theories and interpretations based on distortions through misnaming. Give your assent only to what is *actually* true.

Wisdom Is Revealed Through Action, Not Talk

Don't declare yourself to be a wise person or discuss your spiritual aspirations with people who won't appreciate them. Show your character and your commitment to personal nobility through your actions.

☻─☻─☻

If You Wish to Test Your Endurance, Do It for Yourself, Not for Others

Don't be puffed up with pride if you are able to provide for your needs with very little cost. The first task of the person who wishes to live wisely is to free himself or herself from the confines of self-absorption.

Consider how much more frugal the poor are than we, how much better they forebear hardship. If you want to develop your ability to live simply, do it for yourself, do it quietly, and don't do it to impress others.

⊙-⊙-⊙

Wisdom Depends on Personal Vigilance

Most people don't realize that both help and harm come from within ourselves. Instead they look to externals, mesmerized by appearances.

Wise people, on the other hand, realize that we are the source of everything good or bad for us. They therefore don't resort to blaming and accusing others. They aren't driven to convince people they are worthy or special or distinguished.

If wise people experience challenges, they look to themselves; if they are commended by others, they quietly smile to themselves, unmoved; if they are slandered, they don't feel the need to defend their name.

But they go about their actions with vigilance, assuming that all is well, yet not perfectly secure. They harmonize their desires with life as it is and seek to avoid only the things that would prevent their ability to exercise their will properly. They exercise moderation in all their affairs. And if they seem ignorant or unsophisticated, it is of no concern to them. They know that they only have to watch out for themselves and the direction of their own desires.

☙☙☙

Living Wisdom Is More Important Than Knowing About It

If someone tries to impress you, claiming to understand the writings and ideas of a great thinker such as Chrysippus, think to yourself, the important thing is not to be able merely to talk fluently about abstruse subjects. What is essential is to understand nature and align your intentions and actions with the way things are. The person who truly understands Chrysippus's writings or the precepts of any great mind is the person who actually *applies* the philosopher's teachings. There is a big difference between saying valuable things and doing valuable things.

Don't give too much weight to erudition alone. Look to the example of people whose actions are consistent with their professed principles.

☙☙☙

Learn to Apply Basic Principles to Particular Circumstances in Accordance with Nature

The life of wisdom begins with learning how to put principles, such as "we ought not to lie," into practice. The second step is to demonstrate the truth of the principles, such as why it is that we ought not to lie. The third step, which connects the first two, is to indicate why the explanations suffice to justify the principles. While the second and third steps are valuable, it is the first step that matters most. For it is all too easy and common to lie while cleverly demonstrating that lying is wrong.

Start Living Your Ideals

Now is the time to get serious about living your ideals. Once you have determined the spiritual principles you wish to exemplify, abide by these rules as if they were laws, as if it were indeed sinful to compromise them.

Don't mind if others don't share your convictions. How long can you afford to put off who you really want to be? Your nobler self cannot wait any longer.

Put your principles into practice—now. Stop the excuses and the procrastination. This is your life! You aren't a child anymore. The sooner you set yourself to your spiritual program, the happier you will be. The longer you wait, the more you will be vulnerable to mediocrity and feel filled with shame and regret, because you know you are capable of better.

From this instant on, vow to stop disappointing yourself. Separate yourself from the mob. Decide to be extraordinary and do what you need to do—now.